VOYAGER
TAROT
COMPANION

R. Lloyd Hegland

Foreword by James Wanless

Voyager Tarot Companion © R. Lloyd Hegland 2013
All rights reserved.

Living Dreams Press, Publisher

Cover design by Amy Beth Katz
Cover & Inside Art by James Wanless & Ken Knutsen

Library of Congress Cataloging-in Publication Data
R Lloyd Hegland
  Voyager Tarot Companion—2nd ed.

Library of Congress Control Number:
ISBN-13: 978-0-9890941-4-6

1st ed., First Printing, April 2013.
Color Interior, 194 pages

Living Dreams Press
www.livingdreamspress.com

DEDICATION

I dedicate this book to my family: Del, my brother; Lani, my sister; and especially to my parents Dagmar Cooke Hegland and David Leroy Hegland who dragged me—often kicking and screaming—all over the globe. Despite my initial resistance and confusion, you lovingly and expertly taught me to travel and see all the wonderfully diverse people I met with open, loving eyes. I learned profoundly from all I met along the way and remain deeply grateful for my global schooling. After all, it was only in mastering outer travel that I was able to voyage within and so create this book.

TABLE OF CONTENTS

CUPS 93

WORLDS 123

WANDS 153

FOREWORD BY JAMES WANLESS

Throughout the ages, the Tarot has had the power to inform and inspire. Tarot works because the cards represent a universal wisdom guide—a map of life— and because their archetypal symbols, which are deeply entrenched in human consciousness, are in the form of pictures. Symbolic images command attention at the highest levels of awareness and to our personal subconscious and collective unconscious. Thus, they are the source of all magic: our manifestation ability to realize visions and dreams. Magic is the bloodstream of the universe and so the Tarot continues its irrepressible presence on the human psyche.

In R. Lloyd Hegland's magic spinning of verse to visions and poems to pictures, you experience an exponential impact of the Tarot's power. Putting the Voyager symbolic dreamscapes with words naturally integrate right brain imaginal thinking and left-brain word thinking, so working and playing with the cards becomes a whole brain experience, which is where and when the alchemy of creation happens.

Lloyd is a true voyager, having traveled worldwide starting at an early age, and over the years, he has become an adept Voyager Tarot reader and seer. Combining his curiosity as a seeker with a Bachelor's degree in English, Lloyd has brought to light in words the essential meanings of the cards. As the creator of Voyager, it is a wonder to see another evoke the cards through the medium of language. We are all interpreters of life. Everything is a Tarot, and Lloyd has captured that understanding. This work takes the Tarot beyond the rather tedious and old explanations of cards into the realm of spontaneous origination. It activates the deep knowings of our archetypal consciousness so that we "remember" ourselves – who we are and who we are meant to be. As Plato once said, enlightenment is a process of remembering. It takes a powerful tool to unlock and awaken this primordial treasure box of awareness. This book is a catalyst to our innate knowing.

In this world of information overload – images and images, words and words – it's difficult to cull out what is of lasting value. What sticks and stays within us stimulates the thinking-mind while at the same time sparking the heart to have emotional and transformational affect. So, as I read the picture-words by Lloyd here about the Moon Card I just picked, I sense and remember not all the details, but the big feeling of my emotional "tides and inner beauty."

Emotions are the energizers that move us and keep us moving and that's precisely what these Tarot word-images elicit from deep within ourselves. Beauty and art are evidenced here, and these aesthetic expressions touch us in a way that just a picture or just some written instructions and definitions do not. Getting lost in the barrage of information, we lose our way of "walking in beauty." This book recovers and restores the magic of the Tarot journey. We rediscover here the voyage of life as being a process of passion and joy and elegance.

Pick a card and read these poetic portals into the mystery of consciousness. This process is like walking through a divine doorway into the light for walking your way of destiny. Enlightened and

empowered by this bridge to the soul, you are
inexorably called and pulled by your destined future.
Thank you Lloyd.

~ James Wanless, January 15, 2013

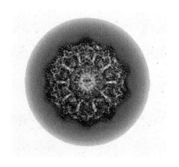

www.thelivingfuture.org
www.voyagertarot.com

INTRODUCTION

TAROT FOR THE 21ST CENTURY:

The Voyager Tarot deck was created by Dr. James Wanless and illustrated by Ken Knutson. James is a brilliant Tarot proponent for many reasons, but he broke the mold by making Tarot fun, light and open. Gone is the dusty arcane medieval obtuseness so often associated with Tarot cards; instead, his Voyager deck is thoroughly contemporary and accessible. For almost thirty years, the Voyager Tarot has helped sitters fully follow and understand the cards as the reading unfolds so that they too become active and fully conscious participants in the wisdom spread out before them, rather than being the passive and confused observers of most other decks. With their photographed collage cameos we are drawn into the cards' vistas and can always identify with and feel the images in the layout before us. Voyager Tarot is indeed a modern and extremely useful guide for 21st century living. It has transformed my life profoundly as it has transformed the lives of hundreds of thousands of others. Voyager Tarot will be with us for many decades to come, taking us on voyages of the Spirit.

ORIGIN OF THIS BOOK

I started writing poems specifically about Tarot three years ago. I'd just started my Facebook page and was eager to give a different and even deeper slant to the Voyager Tarot cards to light the way for others. Tarot is deeply symbolic. I'd learned as an English major that poetry is the language of symbols, as it is also the language of the soul.

No one else that I knew of was writing about Tarot poetically, so I started selecting daily cards and writing poems about them. First I wrote Haiku-like mini poems. As my confidence and competence grew, I embellished and grew them into this style:

<u>Courage: The Spirit of the Chariot</u>
Courage is a torch in the darkness
of our Future:
Light it!

Later, they evolved into something like:

<u>Passion: Emotion of Fortune</u>
When Hierophant has struck
and dragged out stale sadness
passion can wash the soggy old
in fires and steams of Gold.

Soon, I was getting recognition as more and more friends "liked" my Facebook page and commented that they really understood the cards better, grokking them deeper and richer. Symbols are linguistic tools which harken and draw us into deeper waters which cannot be as well plumbed with the shallower tools of prose. Poetry shakes our careful constructions and allows the structure to be reconfigured; rebuilt anew. I was also gaining a profound deepening of my own understanding of the cards. It was like walking around a sculpture and seeing all its aesthetic bounty rather than just staying on the well-walked path down the middle of the museum hall.

My dear friend Treysii, who at the time was also my coach, soon recommended that I expand my mini-tarot poems and start poetically defining each card in the Voyager Tarot deck. Before starting, I knew I needed an emotional purging: to cut myself from the old rotting moorings and allow the currents of my soul's impulse to create my new path. I paddled far out on my surfboard and entered the emotional waters...

<u>Illumination: The Spirit of the Magician</u>
When Nurturing has dried,
And fruit lies dusty
Ecstasy can fill your Spirit
With sweet new Nectar
like a Magician!
♥

I initially named my Tarot poems the *Energy of Voyager Tarot* because the cards, like everything else in our universe, are made up of energy. Further, I believed that each and every one of the 78 cards in the deck had its own unique and eternal energy, or what Rupert Sheldrake calls a "morphic resonance." In simple terms, this is a memory of the past. It is type of consistent energetic pattern. It also encapsulated my intention of delving deeper into each card's meaning, message and power. After three long and challenging years I finally completed all 78 poems; one for each card in the Voyager Tarot deck. I'm deeply honored to present them to you here.

My core intention was and remains to add human warmth and dimension to Tarot; to cut into the depth of each embellished, cardboard card so that the axiomatic truths of humanity—our wishes, dreams and strengths—can be seen by all. My wish was, and remains, to make the cards real, vibrant and alive within us all, all the way from our deepest red blood cells to our highest ascendant indigo spirits, and to join them together through the words and cadence that came to me in the vibrant eternal robes of Soul. I want them to stand out and live as archetypes. After all, we are all on a virgin voyage into our greatest potential from our deepest past. We are all like the *Fool Child* starting out ever anew, naive but trusting on his soul journey...

WHO WILL BENEFIT FROM THIS BOOK?

The poems were originally written with the readers and followers of James Wanless's Voyager Tarot deck in mind. However, while the imagery and wording are built on and from this wonderful deck, I believe that the poems addcto the understanding of *all* Tarot. Just as my extensive library of Tarot decks and books have influenced and helped me write these poems, so my intention has always been to add to the vast body of wisdom known as Tarot. My deepest intent is that these poems contribue to the collective wisdom of all my fellow lovers of Tarot.

This book is also intended as an introduction to Tarot for those dabbling in or perhaps newly drawn to this genre. These poems are intended to guide you into the essence of each card faster and deeper than more prosaic explanations.

Finally these poems could be a wonderful bedside addition, a poetic preparation for sleep and dreams, a catalyst for our day's end-thoughts, reflections and reminiscences.

WHY ME?

There is a wonderful ancient Chinese blessing which goes, "May you live in interesting times." When I look back over my life, this adage seems to fit mine perfectly. If we create our own reality, as I believe we do, I really created an interesting life

I was born to a young American couple in Sweden shortly after World War II. Mom and Dad were deeply in love, brimming with beauty and intelligence and eager for travel and adventure. I remember that Mom wore a beautiful sterling silver heart-shaped locket. Inscribed on its top were the words "The world is a book and those who stay at home read only the cover." Through their spirit and actions—really throughout their entire lives—they together epitomized every word of that quote. My own life later followed suit.

Dad had joined General Motors as an aspiring executive and his first overseas assignment towards exploring and experiencing that goal was to Stockholm Sweden, where my brother and I were born. My sister Lani was born five years later in Belgium. Sweden became the first of twelve countries I lived in and dozens that I visited. By the time I was thirteen, I'd lived in seven countries, each with a different language, and had been a student in five completely different educational systems. Dad's career blossomed and as his position advanced, we moved. He became Managing Director of General Motors: first in Denmark, then South Africa, Australia and later England. It seemed he was being groomed for the top position in General Motors international. Mom was his perfect partner and eagerly complemented his corporate genius.

This dramatic upbringing had a profound and lasting effect on my outlook and attitudes. I remember as a young teenager asking the universe for "experience". Well, it sure came through and supplied me with experience in bounteous amounts! Eventually, I returned to America and finished my high school and then university with a major in English literature and minors in philosophy and psychology. A liberal arts education suited me well and ideally aided my path into many varied fields. When I returned to Australia I had a plethora of career experiences. I worked on Aussie ranches, in the fishing industry, construction and Aussie pubs and hotels. I owned and ran a hippie, sterling silver gift shop called *The Silver Cave*; owned and ran a rural delicatessen/butcher shop called *The Tender Joint* and eventually managed a commercial laundry in the tropics called *The Clean Inn*. When I returned to USA in 1992 to rejoin my family in fabulous Santa Barbara, I again traveled extensively in the West, survived five fishing/processing trips in the Bering sea and eventually became a tour guide/operator based in Santa Barbara, CA with a tour company called *Blue Sky Tours*. It was during that period that I discovered what was to become my greatest love – Tarot, and in particular, the gorgeous Voyager Tarot. This culminated in my Tarot reading business, *On The Path Tarot*.

These varied and fluxuating experiences taught me invaluable lessons. They taught me trust and bravery. I learned to just plunge into exciting new fields and situations, unconcerned with trifles— like knowing anything about what I was getting into! I trusted, from an early age. I just knew that life had purpose and meaning. I knew that I was never alone and that I was being supported and held by both visible *and* invisible but powerful friends.

The people I met in all their multitudes of talents gave me my most important learning lessons.

Through them I was able to discover living humanity with all it's rich dramatic hue and vibrant meaning and see those qualities reflected in the Tarot cards. The cards became almost alive as I saw in them myself and all those I met. They were like the glass beads in my life's rosary, each integral to all I became. In the words of Ralph Waldo Emerson; "Dream delivers us to dream, and there is no end to illusion. Life is like a train of moods, like a string of beads, and, as we pass through them, they prove to be many-colored lenses which paint the world their own hue." I thank every person I met deeply.

HOW TO USE THIS BOOK

This book should be used to clarify and deepen your connection and understanding of any of the Voyager Tarot cards. You can pick a card if you have this beautiful and highly recommended deck, or simply flip to a page for instant insight, or if you require clarity on cards already selected. Regardless of method, I strongly suggest reading the words and meditating on the visual imagery together, as each adds depth of understanding to the other. I recommend that you first quiet your mind, body and soul. With a deep slow breath, eyes relaxed and slightly unfocused, see the drawn picture. See its elements. Notice its symbols and allow the eyes to be drawn to the features that most attract you. Then, with the images still strong in your mind's eye, slowly, deeply and lovingly turn to the image's poem: its verbal collage.

Imagine looking into an illumined box with the image card clear on the top and the verbal imagery, the energy of poem, underneath and also clear. Now, while remaining centered and still, slowly read the words. Without bias or conscious intent, simply allow the words to spill over you. Let them chill and invigorate you with their clarity, cadence and beat, like a mountain waterfall. Rest in the cascading flow and when the Soul has absorbed the verbal and visual collage together and as one, simply stand back from the waters and silently return within. With a still, small voice ask for the depth to be clarified in the warming waters of meaning. The cards and words together can be used as a meditation. Simply summon the images to speak; ask for clarity on an issue, person or event. Again simply take the combined collages in—ask and listen. Have fun!

ORGANIZATION AND ELEMENTS

The Voyager deck is composed of 78 illustrated cards divided into three main sections: Major Arcana, Minor Arcana and Family, or "Court" cards: Sage, Child, Woman and Man. For the purposes of simplicity and fast reference, this book contains only two main sections: the Major Arcana and the Minor Arcana, which includes the Family cards at the beginning of each suit.

The first section is called "Major Arcana" which means "main secrets." These 22 cards reflect the primary archetypal aspects of human reality and are numbered according to a developmental structure, starting with 0 = *Fool* and ending with *21* = *Universe*. This is essentially a storyline of the human soul's quest for transformation, fullfulment and enlightenment. Another way to grasp the Major Arcana is to consider that human beings are multifaceted jewels. Each of our 22 facets are spectacular holographic aspects of our whole selves.

Some people may experience many of these facets in one lifetime, while others will live through only a few of them. By working with Tarot, we have the potential to consciously master them all.

The second section of this book contains the Family cards, which are akin to Queens, Kings and Jacks in a typical playing card deck. In most modern Tarot decks there are four medieval royal figures each in one of the four suits mentioned above, and thereby equalling sixteen cards. The Voyager Tarot deck, being a contemporary version of an ancient art, uses four familiar archetypes of humanity: Man, Woman, Child and Sage, again defined by the four suits. James Wanless calls these the "Family" cards because together they mirror the family within each of our deeper selves.

The four Man cards indicate masculine energies at work. While they can speak to the presence of an external male in one's life, which is further identified or refined by the suit, Man also symbolizes the qualities of action, directness, extroversion and moving outward into the world in oneself. Everyone, regardless of biology or gender, has both masculine and feminine energies. According to Jungian Psychology and Buddhism, balancing the "yang" of the male with the "yin" of the female is essential to our mental and spiritual health.

The four Woman cards reproduce and reflect the subtle and internal powers: like the moon herself, Woman influence the tides, the internal waters, and reflect intuition, perceptiveness and compassion.

The Child cards speak to the children within us all: the vulnerable, the playful, the sensuous, the adventurous explorers.

The Sage cards reflect the wise ones that carry the wisdom of the ancients forward.

As mentioned above, each of the sixteen Family cards correspond with a particular suit and are included within the "Minor Arcana," or "minor secrets": representations of aspects or emotions of our lives that we all experience, even if only fleetingly, like Love, Disappointment or Brilliance. There are ten cards in each of the four suits.

Cups reflect emotional reality and soul. They are feminine/yin and relate to the element of water. They are represented in the Voyager deck in the symbolism of containers, shells and flowers.

Crystals signify mind or intellect. They are masculine/yang, sharp, smooth, multifacted, useful. They relate to the element of air. In other decks "Swords" is the symbol of this suit.

Wands reflect Spirit. They are feminine/yin and relate to the element of fire. They are represented in the Voyager deck by the symbolism of sticks, rods or staffs.

Worlds are "of the world." Worlds are material, tangible and touchable. They are masculine/yang and relate to the element of Earth. In this deck they are pictured as planets, suns or moons. In most other Tarot Decks they are represented as discs, pentacles and coins (money).

Together, all the cards tell the epic story of humanity and the spiritual quest—the sacred voyage —called life.

Section I: Major Arcana

O

Fool-Child

FOOL-CHILD

0

FOOL-CHILD is birthed in trust.
He goes forth knowing life as Eternal.

FOOL-CHILD adventures into the night
knowing that there is no wrong only right,
brushed in the deep primal faith
that all roads lead Home.

FOOL-CHILD starts from nothing everywhere.
He is the beginning and ending,
the Alpha and Omega.
FOOL-CHILD is the child of all;
FOOL-CHILD is everything and nothing;
FOOL-CHILD is in us all waiting
for All that is.

When FOOL-CHILD card calls you out to voyage,
trust and courage are your luggage
and will always take you back to your goal
wrapped in the soothing arms of an angel.
The Energy of the FOOL-CHILD
is knowing and brave.

It is the foolish wisdom of instinct,
unerringly guiding us on and on;
from birth to birth ever discovering
peace in our next breath,
home in our next step.

FOOL-CHILD is you as I AM.

I

Magician

MAGICIAN

The Magician stands in the Veil:
he is one with both sides;
with his right hand he reaches from Spirit,
with his left hand he gives to Worlds.

His palms are always open and hold his gifts;
with thought he brings his desires forth.

His number "I" stands in the shadow of eternity
and on the edges of infinity.
Magician does not count or wait,
he is the ultimate Man-I-fester.

Magician has four wonderful assistants;
Brilliance for conceiving the desire;
Ecstasy for feeling it take form;
Success for knowing its imminence;
and *Illumination* for constantly growing as "I AM".

When you have the Magician card,
the Universe is at your command,
waiting for your mind to form your wish.
You too at that moment recognize
your Magicianship.
When you have the card all doubt must be set aside:
just ask, with NO doubt, and it will be given.
The energy of Magician is electric,
It is like lightning, glorious fireworks
or an ethereal sunset.
Magician transcends time and space,
It is who you really are .

Priestess

PRIESTESS

II

Priestess lives in her hearing
and sees through all illusion and deceit.
Priestess trusts intimately, feeling like a gentle lover.
She is conduit. Messenger. Circuit.
Priestess speaks from the Divine
straight to the depths of your soul.

Priestess thinks with passionate detachment,
her feelings in balance never jagged or flimsy.
Priestess reflects and speaks with soft strength,
her Spirit is pure like fresh snow,
as clear as a winter breeze.

When you meet the Priestess card on Tarot's path
stop and listen,
withdraw within and wait.
With slow, deep breath,
Spirit will speak and you will hear.
If mind, body and feelings
are like a clear blue iceberg
calmly expect and trust.

The energy of the Priestess card
is calm and still;
as strong as a glacier
as trusting as a raft.

Your Priestess reflects like the Moon
seeing with deep diamond eyes
into hidden Truth.

III

Empress

EMPRESS

III

Empress stands in the fields of Eden,
arms spread she welcomes us in.
She is one with Gaia
ruling through compassion and love.

Protector and Mother,
she brings to bloom the flowers
within us all.
Empress heals our rifts and kisses our wounds.
She sends the white dove with love.

Empress is indivisible: she is prime.
Empress's gifts are creativity,
bringing beauty, synergy and love
into solutions seeing the divine
perfection in us all.

Empress nurtures our growing babies of genius.
She is compassionate, receptive and accepting.

When you behold the Empress card
you are engulfed in love and deep understanding;
your heart opens like a lotus
and allows ALL in.
All become One as you drop judgments;
accepting Divine Mother in all creation.

The energy of Empress is soft and enveloping;
it is strong, warm and inclusive.
Like a willow, Empress bends with the gusts,
and weeps for the emptied.

IV

Emperor

EMPEROR

IV

Emperor is decisive and strong.
Emperor uses logical, direct thinking.
He is quick to anger and refuses doubt.

Emperor aspires to great heights.
He is always commencing new conquests:
never patient, Emperor just acts...

If you have the Emperor card you need to act!
Bring forth your inner Emperor
and reach high:
all is possible.

The energy of the Emperor quivers
in anticipation, and plans
beyond.
Focused, strong, methodical,
it blends forceful passion with will.

As Emperor
fly like an eagle
breach like a whale
fill your appetite at the banquet of Life.

Plan and build:
your empire awaits.

V

Hierophant

HIEROPHANT

∨

The Hierophant is compassionate but stern.
He teaches lessons for Life: big lessons that last.
Hierophant is not concerned with the three "R's".
He teaches lessons that change lives;
lessons that are absorbed deep into the Soul.

As "V" Hierophant is prime and true.
Like dark colors he shades our life.
Hierophant is not the lilies resplendent in the vale
or dappled autumn shades hypnotizing with beauty.
Hierophant teaches through his children:
Oppression teaching to be free and focused;
Disappointment teaching trust and gratitude;
Setback teaching us to believe
and revel in the process;
Negativity teaching us to negate it
with positive love.

When you encounter the Hierophant card,
expect no trivia.
You will remember your homework for aeons.
Life will change hue and the moment is pivotal:
hold your breath then relax into love.

The energy of the Hierophant is stern but fair.
It sees into and changes the course
of your soul.
The energy loves you and knows you
are bigger than your chinks,
stronger than the harsh lessons,
ready to grow.

LOVERS

VI

Lovers are together and alone.
Lovers persist in all seasons:
Lovers are together in spring, autumn, summer and
winter, the dead of night, at high noon, dawn and
sunset Lovers are.

Lovers start from one core,
balancing and embracing all within.
Then and only then can Lovers be plural
and inclusive.

Lovers are divisible by "III" and "II";
Lovers are together with *Empress* and *Priestess*.
The Lover's sign is Gemini, dualistic towards all
even in solitude.

Lovers allow and envelop opposites,
like Yin and Yang
Lovers have the seed of their opposite within.
Lovers dwell in loving contradiction.

The energy of Lovers is enveloping and warm:
it lacks all judgment and is at peace in the arms of
contradiction:
lovers see all as one together.

If you embrace the Lovers card,
you look for balance
and acceptance within
and only then move out.

VII

Chariot

CHARIOT

The Chariot is movement.
He travels with passion towards his goal
impatient as a stallion clawing with hooves,
as eager as a Hawk pulling to soar.

The Chariot is primal and indivisible.
He is Cancer knowing he is his home.

Chariot says
"We shall never cease from exploration
for the end of our exploring would be to
take us where we started
and to see it for the first time."

Chariot explores and moves with his heart,
mind, spirit and his body.

His offspring are *Fear, Dullness, Courage* and
Breakthrough;
Chariot travels fearlessly alone or with them.

When you ride the Chariot card you are restless.
You need to consult a map and find the direction
towards your blissful arrival; of your safe berth.

The energy of the Chariot is restless for completion.
It beckons your inner compass to direct you
Homeward.

VIII

Balance

BALANCE

VIII

Balance is a quest; a dance.
It comes fleetingly on the wings of an in-breath
only to part on the exhale.
It is Impersonal.
It is the sign of infinity upright "8".
Balance is a dancer on a sword;
a hummingbird resting on it's beak.

It is justice searching for validation and YOU
looking for that moment of still peace.

Balance is what we came to find.
It is immortality squeezed into a Moment.

Balance is Justice for all as a projection from within.
Its energy is stable but fleeting;
eager but sober.
piercing and unbiased.

Balance speaks from the mind, heart, body and
Spirit as ONE voice:
we all yearn to hear and speak as a whole.

The "Children" of Balance
are *Stagnation* and *Change*,
Synthesis and *Harmony*.

When you steady yourself on the Balance Card
excavate your inner pyramid.
Take the chance to equalize all your aspects
on a higher level.

IX

Hermit

HERMIT

IX

The Hermit covets the darkness and the light.
He is inner and outer
as deep as a well,
and as light as a feather.

Hermit dwells in the eye of the hurricane,
still as Buddha amidst change,
prophet, sage and seller of silent
strength.

Hermit is deep in his cave strolling down
Madison Avenue;
Hermit shops in the higher realms
coveting nothing, owning all within.

Hermit breaths in *fulfillment*
in his delicate strong *balance*;
he gathers his earned fruits as sweet *harvest*.
Hermit is complete under the cathedral dome
of his *integrity*.

If you receive the gift of the Hermit card
your beckoning cave is safe and warm.
Your hermit will balance your inner and outer
as you have masterfully balanced
your upper and lower.
As Above so below; as within so without.
Still and calm,
Hermit resonates "Salem," "Ahoo" and "Namaste."
Hermit swirls in the opposites as Yin AND Yang.

X

Fortune

FORTUNE

×

Fortune teems in the Universe:
the "horn of plenty" is everywhere
and in everything.

Fortune is a ferris wheel
turning like karma, rising and ebbing like the tides.

Fortune is the apogee and the perigee,
the accepting and denying, the opening and closing.

Fortune has four shades:
Delusion beckons you to your vision;
Passion urges you on, closer and closer;
Reward arrives home;
Growth results.

This is the moment when surety is critical.
Accept your abundant right and bring your riches
forth with NO doubt.
Be the jeweled black Madonna, the ruby peacock
and the golden firework.

The energy of the Fortune card is resplendent and
inevitable.
It glistens with presence and hearkens from within.
Fortune has the energy of compassion:
it sees itself in all things, especially YOU.
Allow the birth of your own Fortune;
be the Golden butterfly, the glittering palm saying
"I AM Fortune incarnate."

XI

Strength

STRENGTH

Strength is feline and flexible.
Its gaze can kill or bless.
Strength is within us all stalking our doubts;
Strength can stretch and purr
or pounce and wound.

As XI, Strength is prime and indivisible;
Strength cannot be divided or split, it is fearless
purity.
It is one with *Priestess II*, a psychic master and
student.
Strength has no children but is eternal and waiting,
Always with us and ready.

The energy of Strength is trans-formative.
It takes you in its teeth and pulls you from your
cocoon.

It breaths life into your wings and companions you
on your journeys.

Strength is older than the Parthenon,
as primal as Fire.

When you have the Strength Card you briefly
become immortal,
a God who cannot fail or doubt.

Use the card well,
it is power.

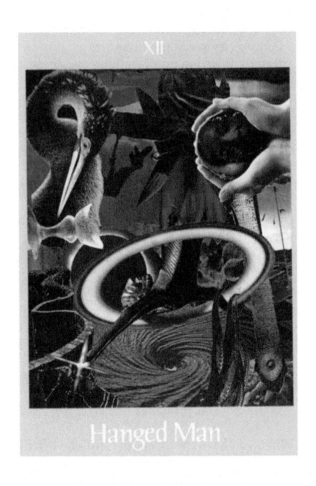

HANGED MAN

XII

Hanged Man waits
and waits and waits ...
for the answer to come to HIM.

Hanged Man is Odin upside down waiting
seeing all from a new perspective.
Hanged Man is Jesus being a new way of seeing,
Jesus being new so we could grow too.

Hanged Man is a reflection of ourselves
in the darkness of our shadow;
seeing in a palm held shell our true face.

Hanged man is the fish waiting for the heron strike.
Hanged Man is the target ring suspended
as we are drawn by the swirling tar.

When the Hanged Man card drops into your life
you have potential building and all could come.
You are most at odds with *Patience* and her friends
Trust, *Love* and *Faith*.

Hanged Man is alone but loves
VI *Lovers*, IV *Emperor* and III *Empress*.

Hanged Man waits to be lowered head first
into the tarry swirl, that black whirlpool
into the universal sea.

XIII

Death

DEATH

Death is the hollow mask peering;
the sceptered gown waiting
for flesh filled return.

Death is the tide turn, the forest burn
the heron strike, the turtle bite.

Death is the end of the river;
the beginning of the brook.

Death is never final;
Death is transformational, not terminal.
Death is a lobster under a rock
growing a bigger shell.

When the Death card comes calling
it summons you to your cocoon;
it tells you to rest and summon strength
to take a break so you can Grow.

Death hearkens change,
it summons you for Preparation.

Ignoring Death is futile,
Death finds you.
Make Death your friend
and it will serve you, always.

ART

XIV

Art is an alchemical energy bubbling up
from within us all.

Art is the reorganization
into an ordered higher form.

The energy of Art is creative;
seeing beauty and form in what may otherwise
seem formless,
meaningless and bland.

Art is water and light creating a rainbow
or coal and pressure creating a diamond.

Art is the Human expression of our divinity;
it is the imposition of our will
to translate to a higher plane
that which might otherwise remain
chaotic.

When you draw the Art card
you have the potential
of introducing beauty into a situation
and re-forming your perspective to it.

The energy of Art is poised and latent,
able to transpose a "leaden" jumble
into gold.

XV

Devil's Play

DEVIL'S PLAY

XV

Devil's Play is the Law of celebration in action;
it is saturnine discipline hidden under purple velvet;
it is the giggling laughter at obedience denied;
It is dancing in the rain
or galloping with moonlight.

Devil's Play is flagons and flutes; jazz and circles.
Devil's Play is you and me together
in drumbeat revelry.

Devil is being lived in the opposite
like yalping is to play
uncoiled and loose.
It is the reinvention and the recharge.

Devil's Play is a dance
between *Empress III* and *Hierophant V*:
finding compassion on the high wire overlooking
stern Lessons.

When the Devil's Play card knocks on your door
loosen your tie or girdle, play and celebrate
your victories without restraint.
Let crusty morning set you back to tasks set aside
by night's wanton revelry.

The energy of Devil's Play is relaxed and free.
It reverses your marching beat and allows
fire and music to dance you
in Dionysian delight.

TOWER

XVI

Tower is the cleanser, the stripper.
Tower is an instant alchemy,
purifying the old and tearing away the dead.
Tower is death without a cocoon;
instantly transmuting lead to gold.
Tower is as merciful as fire
as compassionate as gravity.

Tower XVI has three supporting relatives;
Balance VIII who works behind the scenes;
Emperor IV who guards the process
from all four quadrants;
Priestess II who guides the process.

If you climb the Tower card
be prepared for sudden change;
in moments your world will transform
and your "dead parts" burnt away
in your Soul's fierce cauldron.
Tower says the universe is no longer nudging you.
Universe has waited and now pushes you
off the Tower of ego.

The energy of Tower is uncompromising and strong.
It is a revolutionary cleansing, a burning away.
Tower never consults or waits: Tower does.

Tower is an instant rebirth to a higher plane.
Never resist Tower or Tower grows higher.
The energy of Tower will change your lead to gold;
in great gratitude, hold on.

XVII

Star

STAR

Star radiantly shines.
Star need not DO but lives in BEING.
Star knows her magnificent radiance;
Star stands still and attracts all.

All look to Star forgetting that they are no less.
Star is the prime, alone, turning others on
to their own brilliant perfection.

Star is knowing that being all we are
is sufficient.

When the Star card shines upon you,
recognize and honor
your deep glowing magnificence.
See yourself as others and others as you;
in sweet silky jade.
Like Kwan Yin
compassionately pour liquid love over all others:
anoint them.

The energy of Star is magnificent but still.
Star is you twinkling in the deepest part,
eager to emerge.

Star stands radiant,
in galaxies of many.

Star is you humbly
growing.

XVIII

Moon

MOON

Moon is patient and reflects,
feeling and moving the tides.
Moon caresses the Earth
dancing gently with her.

Moon is calm and deep.
She hides her deep beauty under colorless dust.
She draws you into your inner Moon.
She speaks to your tides and inner beauty,

Moon is sensual as a dream,
as polished as an uncut diamond.

Moon feels beyond the here and now.
She knows from within,
book-less but real and wise.

When the Moon card shines upon you
your dreams speak louder,
your tides are sharper
and your feelings are richer.
Watch your Owl,
hear your Wolf.

The energy of the Moon is sensitive and passive,
dark and reflective; intuitive and sensual.
She reaches for color and heat.
Beware of over passivity, still breathe and act!

Moon and Sun balance each other.

XIX

Sun

SUN

Sun is liquid gold, glistening from within.
Sun is fields of flowers swaying in soft breezes.

When Sun sets, be ready for voluptuous dreams,
sumptuous feasts and quivering love.

Sun is a monarch butterfly flying
bravely over a continent and passing sweetly
over the gentle face of a Pharaoh's child.

Sun is bullion sprinkled friendships and
hand-held golden love.

Sun is alone and together; complete.
He heats with desire; burns with unity.
Sun as XIX draws you in to your fire:
Sun burns the trivial and torches the empty.

When you shine with the Sun card
your moment has come.
Climb your pedestal and accept your medal;
with deep humility love your arrival
and honor your journey.

The energy of the Sun card is powerful and warm.
It is Tutankhamen softly gazing towards eternity
knowing that he will arrive when Infinity
with sandy shoes
has come.

XX

Time-Space

TIME-SPACE (KARMA)

XX

Time-Space is an echo of a distant drum beat;
its beat winding up your hidden canyon walls
reminding you of past commitments, still unkept
and patterns drawn on your sandy shores.

Time-Space has many, many offspring:
She, as Karma, is like the pebble thrown
in a deep, deep pond;
Her ripples never end.
She is found in all lives and numbers.

Time-Space repeats and repeats in your ear until
you undo the source
and move beyond.

When you have the Time-Space card
your "echo" is near;
and you must again deal with and spin away from
the mesmerizing drum beat pattern
of your many lives,
Not as a mental decision alone
but with your entire being.

The energy of Time-Space is insistent but subtle;
she offers you a glimpse beyond to the universe
and offers growth to leave the dead leaves
of your past.
Time-Space is a gyre spinning you higher
and beyond;
back to YOU now,
here and new.

XXI

Universe

UNIVERSE

The Universe is growing!
It has limitless potential.
The Universe reaches in all directions
from all things
it is the Alpha AND Omega.

The Universe is bubbling,
it churns in growth.

It must decide
where do I grow next?
What choice
is next?

If you are circling 'round the Universe card,
you have growth given in all directions.

BUT you must chose; prioritize.
Be a master of one, then another, then another.
Don't be a "Jack" and fritter away potential,
by a spinning growth.
Be focused.

The energy of the Universe card
is bubbling with unfocused potential.
It is a masterpiece
uncompleted;
human DNA evolving
brilliant new strands.

"We shall not cease from exploration
And the end of all our exploring
Will be to arrive where we started
And know the place for the first time."

~ T. S. Eliot

Section II: Minor Arcana

CRYSTALS

Knower

Sage of Crystals

SAGE OF CRYSTALS

"KNOWER"

Sage of Crystals sees
through hazy starlight.
He is an observer looking down,
knowing what is,
like seeing lines and wrinkles
on your palm
or light breaking up
through prism.

The Knower has no doubts.
Knower marries all his powers
funneling all through his crystal mind
seeing only what IS.

When the Knower card sparkles in your eyes
pass beyond all uncertainty
into your cave of clarity;
see and love your gleaming Truth.
Complexity will crumble into the dust
of well traveled paths.

The energy of Sage of Crystals,
is absolute and clear.
Knower is calmly sure.
Knower sees what IS
under needlessly turbulent seas
of doubt.

Learner

Child of Crystals

CHILD OF CRYSTALS

"LEARNER"

Child of Crystals is awash in awe,
eyes bursting with fascination,
face glowing with curiosity
of fingers, crystals, numbers and books.

Learner begins slowly
collecting knowledge.
Child of Crystals does not confuse
by multiplying;
Child of Crystals simply sees
the axioms whirling.
He sees light reflecting
off wondrous shapes;
And prisms of light
dividing colors.

If you play with the Child of Crystals card,
your initiation is beginning
and you will visit
the Temple of Awe
where devoted, you begin
our lessons.
Put aside complications and reverently continue
your path into the Sacred Library.

The energy of the Child of Crystals card
is glowing, strong and electric.
You as Learner grow steadily with small steps;
piece by piece you carefully assemble
the puzzle of your life.

Guardian

Woman of Crystals

WOMAN OF CRYSTALS

"GUARDIAN"

Guardian protects with icy will
swirling swarms of diamond jewels.
Her fingers offer a stargate
to faceted caves
and opal walls long sought.
She draws you in
and manifests on alchemical sill
bringing forth form from thought.

Guardian secretly creates.

When graced with the Guardian card,
protect your thoughts.

With Gypsy queen stealth
bring forth your dreams
wrapped in the living luster
of mudra loves long sought.

The energy of Woman of Crystals
is sharp and rich, deep and pure.
Guardian summons glittering gems
through focused power,
and shamanic showers.

Guardian is Peace in turmoil;
calm surrounded by
swirling frenzy sought.

Guardian is the "I" of your Hurricane.

Inventor

Man of Crystals

MAN OF CRYSTALS

"INVENTOR"

The Inventor dances with thoughts
leading and following their beat;
Inventor like a crystal refracts light
and decodes the messages within.
Like channeled waters teeming with life
Man of Crystals receives and uses light
from above discovering gems
in the al-chemistry.

Inventor pulls in from the right
and creates into the left.
Inventor channels and makes.

When you discover the "Inventor Card"
expect answers to come subtly
wrapped and needing assembling.

The energy of Man of Crystals is etheric—
it encodes the colors and scrambles them.

The Energy of Inventor is lateral and indirect;
hiding its wizardry in code,
using riddles and puns
to hide it's gifts
within.

Brilliance

Ace of Crystals

ACE OF CRYSTALS

"BRILLIANCE"

Brilliance is your lightening
lighting up your chakras;
it is a mental tsunami drenching you
in sudden summer soaking showers
which drown your dried lands
and soften the seeds of your waiting fields
into crystal flowers.

Brilliance is the striking of magical chords
of your personal orchestra,
transforming the waiting strings
into a perfect Sonata.

Brilliance is the mind of a magician
turning aeonic wait into crystalline slate
and instant revelation
where anything can be composed.

If you are struck with the Brilliance card,
relax.
Allow magical thoughts to flash and shine
laser light across your path
transforming your destination
into Shambala.

The energy of the Ace of Crystals
is sudden and bold,
bright and clear.
It is sharp and engaging,
blending logic and intuition
into the harmonics of cathartic truth.

Equanimity

Two of Crystals

TWO OF CRYSTALS

"EQUANIMITY"

The mind of the priestess called Equanimity,
is as still as a cloud,
as pregnant as rain.

It is soft like a sapphire seeing all
through prisms of rainbow
steel.

Inpenetrable and calm,
Equanimity lives in truth.
It is a mountain peak knowing
that the sun will warm it's snowy surface.

If you draw the Equanimity card,
be still and sure.

Listen deeply
and truth will ring bells of certainty
within.

The energy of the Two of Crystals
is strong, clear,
impenetrable.
It is sapphire cut to reflect
our deepest secrets
then hidden
in a mountain
of tranquility.

Creativity

Three of Crystals

THREE OF CRYSTALS

"CREATIVITY"

Creativity lives in paradox.

It bursts from the mind in crystal splendor
but flows like a river through emotional passes.
It wells from within like an ancient stranger
yet rests in our belly like a lotus growing.

Creativity is the chemist with a vial,
adding gold dust to our dreams
and blending colors for our prisms
like a rainbow in a beaker.

Creativity is the *Empress* mind;
accepting all as equal,
creating for the whole.

When the Creativity card knocks on your door,
prepare a space for Spirit to visit,
and an honored guest will come
gentle as a gust listening
or a wave unasked
kissing your shore.

The energy of the Creativity card
is sudden as a breeze,
and transformative
as a sweet colored prayer.

The Empress mind
humbly asks for entrance.

Logic

Four of Crystals

FOUR OF CRYSTALS

"LOGIC"

The logical mind is an Emperor
dividing,
conquering and analyzing all.
With sullen determination he hears the call
and leans left dissecting
his empire,
his all.

The *Empress* is on his right
balancing logic with inner sight,
adding inner wisdom to his cold clarity
like fire on a cold crisp night
or dreams of rich clear insight.

The energy of logic is cool but clear
like diamonds on a tender hand
or navigating on a stormy night
with trusting compass
guiding you home.

When the logic card pierces your consciousness
set emotions aside and calmly look
searching in the dark, dusty nooks
for sudden gleaming answers
and the clarifying crystal side
of puzzles' key.

Logic is the Emperor
of your guiding sight,
your team together.

Negativity

Five of Crystals

FIVE OF CRYSTALS

"NEGATIVITY"

Like the shadow of a mighty oak
or a mountain's darkened lofty peak
all light is surrounded by black, by bleak
and illuminates the doubting dark
red pentagon resting in our doubting speech.

Look beyond, trust the sound
of the little inner voice
booming bright
full of light, behind the darkness.

The energy of negativity
is stark and empty
till you stand aside and gaze into its soul
and just negate the negative bowl.

When confronted with the Negativity card
ascend above your thoughts
and focus on all the good you've bought.
Through focus turn
all attacking wasps
into butterflies and hummingbirds
of gratitude
lifting you higher into heaven's ward.

Turn dark to light
intending that delight.

Confusion

Six of Crystals

SIX OF CRYSTALS

"CONFUSION"

thoughts thinking
minds drinking
nectar minds inner spinning
lovers thoughts multiply
in spiral rainbow crystals
like flowers in a vase
or lions behind base bars
lovers mind engorges thoughts
in doubts of love's heart sought
and Spirit's search for wisdom's sight

the mind of lovers denies clarity
the energy of the confusion card
is powerfully diffuse
intensely scattered
a furnace of thoughts
a cauldron of mental shots

when the confusion card confuses you
prepare to be engulfed by herds
of wild mustang thoughts
galloping through tenders sought
the mind of lovers asks for calm
in spiritual emotional balm
surrender your logical mind
and let your spirit enjoy
the wild ride

Dullness

Seven of Crystals

SEVEN OF CRYSTALS

"DULLNESS"

The energy of Seven of Crystals is methodical.
It sweeps the horizon
and turns carefully.
No explosive emotions
or plasma spirit
just mind slowly pulling the reins
of the *Chariot*
thinking and changing mind to match;
the turning bands of time.

If you dredge up the Dullness card,
look at your beliefs and thoughts.
Slowly shift them to the NOW,
leaving in the wake of your *Chariot* dust
thoughts of then and when.

The energy of "Dullness"
is solid,
balanced as a cube,
steady as granite.

With no flashes, no luminants,
the mind of the *Chariot*
steadily draws you
to this moment's finest
thought.

Let it.

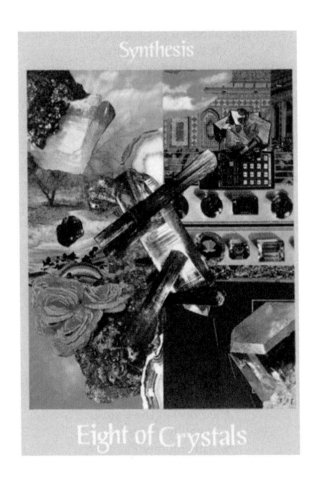

Eight of Crystals

EIGHT OF CRYSTALS

"SYNTHESIS"

Synthesis is the gathering the joining
in crystalline patterns and tribal beat.
Synthesis connects the different
and climbs up to *Balance's* mental seat.

Synthesis is the mental soup;
a brilliant mix of simmering love.
A aerie puzzle, a jangled jigsaw,
a blending to the higher
from the base.

The energy of Synthesis is
hard and tempered; smooth but tight.
Synthesis, like a mental kaleidoscope,
adds to all with crystal light.

When you come together with the Synthesis card,
breath in the quadrants and allow
mental stirring to bring all together
strong as a clear alloy,
smooth as a rainbow.

Allow opposites to attract and gel into more,
with Synthesis'
sweet sharp
delicate
spoor.

Narrowness

Nine of Crystals

NINE OF CRYSTALS

"NARROWNESS"

Focus is the purpose of the Hermit's thought
like swimming is to fish
or feathers from a bird
that aims to fly up to skies long sought.
Hermit thinks with narrow focus
like a laser.

When life befuddles
and swampy watered emotions bubble and foam
eliminate the weeds
and focus on the seed of undulating thought
till crimson clear
it comes.

The energy of Narrowness
is as sharp as a razor
cutting floss relentlessly
clearing jungles of mossythoughts
into fields of
emerald grass.

When you grow the Narrowness card
eliminate the dross and like a Hermit
clear all but the critical
like water to a stone.

Narrowness focuses the mind
and creates the latest sound.

Delusion

Ten of Crystals

TEN OF CRYSTALS

"DELUSION"

Diamond studded dreams on sandy wastes
like leering doubts of dear loves waiting.
Delusion is our vision seen as doubt.
Crystal candy leading us
past broken glass derision
and inner whispered doubts.

Delusion creates palaces
from gossamer splendor.

When you unveil the Delusion card,
throw away the doubts of others
like useless shards and climb
ten ton sandstone boulders
to the summit of your pyramid dreams.
Cross the wastes,
follow your Star.

The energy of Delusion is beckoning but fragile.

Delusion draws you onwards,
seeing dreams as magnets,
luring us through our wastelands,
to promised scapes within.

Delusion is *Fortune* mind drawing you
into your fulfilled dreams.

CUPS

Regenerator

Sage of Cups

SAGE OF CUPS

"REGENERATOR"

Regenerator rebuilds by allowing
flowing waters to sweep
stagnant, blocked emotions
like flowers after spring showers
or lovers crying in reborn Love.

Moving the stuck rebuilds the new,
bringing smiles to craggy faces
like tumbling, bubbling waters
churning down granite cliffs,
falling freely.

If you have the Regenerator card,
allow old waters to flow freely again.

Feel the surging relief of sunlight striking
through and giving again
bright prism colors
and sweet new delights.

Allow emotional *Sage* to rebuild
your lavender sweet emotions.

The energy of Regenerator relentlessly cuts
through granite walls of denial
sweeping the old and birthing anew,
flowing ever to your ocean
reborn.

Feeler

Child of Cups

CHILD OF CUPS

"FEELER"

Child of Cups exudes instantly without filters.
She feels love, sadness, anger
and all other emotions
without editing or diving back to old wounds,
or borrowing from trophies past.
Feeler never imposes the "then" on the "now!"

Feeler feels like chalk on a blackboard
or fingers snaking down your spine.

Feeler has no history but reacts instantly
to her emotional waters,
swimming like Dolphin,
grinning like Cat.

When you dive into the Feeler card
sense your immediacy,
react only to what is.
Allow no past
to insinuate itself
into the now.

The energy of Child of Cups is
as simple as arithmetic
and as natural as a spring shower
blessing blossoms
And filling Ponds.

Rejoicer

Woman of Cups

WOMAN OF CUPS

"REJOICER"

Woman of Cups is in love with life.

Emotions flow through her being
easily.
Woman of Cups rejoices and dances
in the tides of life and knows
that feeling life
is living life.

When you gaze into the face of the Woman of Cups
your brimming emotions must not be blocked
or doubted.
Let the rain fall over you
and in dancing delight grow
your next seeds
in your tears.

You now know that pain and joy
are only drops in the infinite ocean of life.

The energy of "Rejoicer" is receptive and accepting.
It is the shell, flower and cup
waiting in trust to be filled.

The "Rejoicer" is Shiva
celebrating her creation.

Surfer

Man of Cups

MAN OF CUPS

"SURFER "

Man of cups glides over the waters
riding the mountainous cliffs,
sliding gracefully across their crests
until slammed by waters
denied.

Surfer keeps his emotions at bay.
He bravely rides them,
watching them build,
until towering,
they burst upon him as a flower,
drenching him in weeping
perfumes
and cathartic
transformation.

When you meet the Man of Cups,
Surf your emotions and wait.
Bravely prepare for the ideal time,
knowing that the swells could grow
to dangerous heights.

The energy of Man of Cups
is nimble, patient, objective.

Surfer waits for the perfect time
to burst forth
in roaring passion.

Ecstasy

Ace of Cups

ACE OF CUPS

"ECSTASY"

Streaming pollen bursting bitter bright
stamens beckoning fragrant
delights
like clear chilly waters tumbling
in reckless rush as butterfly wings
or humbling sweet spring picnic wind
like blood red joy
of ecstatic heights.

The energy of ecstasy is petal power sweet
like whispered loves silky satin sounds
or sugared chocolate
cream tart rounds.

When the ecstasy card chooses you to seduce
expect Magician to shake your heart
as earthquake rumbles rips apart
sad old dreams of lonely nights
and flings you
into the arms of love.

When ecstasy comes
rejoice in Spirit's
earthly face.

Equilibrium

Two of Cups

TWO OF CUPS

"EQUILIBRIUM"

Priestess emotion soft and steady
floating over the inner waves and
smothering them in damping love
with surfer feathers crossing above
river floating below
always buoyant
always ready.

The energy of equilibrium
is tranquil, steady and sure,
with balsa feathers and cactus
clear intention takes her down
to the ocean
from icy lofty climb.

When you receive the Equilibrium card
soften your emotions and float
with them like a priestess
from jagged mental peaks
to the ocean below.

Maintain emotional balance
despite all float float floating
watery halls.

Love

Three of Cups

THREE OF CUPS

"LOVE"

Like a river of flowers
love flows in glowing fragrance
calming the fighters
and bathing their wounds
in sweet soft embrace.

Love fills all dark corners
and rounds stark edges.
Love melts sharp steel
and eases broken glass
into goblets gleaming class.

The energy of love is warm and soft.
Like a ruby rose, love
soothes the flesh
and stirs the spirit.

It cleanses the old
and sweeps the dross.

When the love card calls,
drop your defenses and lower your arms.
Allow it entrance to your inner altar
and rest in its emotional glow.

Let love conquer you,
flowing in and out
like an emotional tide
on the ocean of Spirit.

Anger

Four of Cups

FOUR OF CUPS

"ANGER"

Anger is as neutral as air,
determined as a whirling hawk
and as fierce as a raging bull.
Anger is the Emperor exclaiming,
"Do It NOW!
or a child screaming for love.

Anger can shatter goblets
or heat the molding glass.
Anger is Pele forming islands;
a trumpet in a sonata
silencing violin choirs.

When the Anger card shakes you awake
be the Emperor and demand;
be the child and grow.
Let your emotions find their home
in fields of scalded grass
and trunks of blackened shock.

The energy of the Anger card
is uncompromising;
like a smoking field
of lava blowing
Pele's kiss.

Disappointment

Five of Cups

FIVE OF CUPS

"DISAPPOINTMENT"

Expected dreams shattered
like sharp broken goblets
littering the floor or
alabaster doorway
sealed and blocked.

Disappointed dead rose blossoms
show the path selected not given
and open gates gleaming
neglected not seen
as eyes pursue in teary gloom
the littered dream long sought.

The energy of disappointment
is spent and tired,
silly and pointless.

Disappointment is as stubborn as a tired mule
as rewarding as a wisp of smoke.

When you have the disappointment card
look beyond and around your dreams:
see the beckoning paths glimmering
and rich.

The universe has seen beyond your hopes
and delivered better.
Thank disappointment
and grow.

Sorrow

Six of Cups

SIX OF CUPS

"SORROW"

Black ink octopus tears
glistening on tarnished eyes
like sandy shores and salted fears
of loving loves lost
but alive.

Sorrow is the emptying of remembrance;
a Grecian tragedy spilled in rending pain.

Sorrow is the perceived ripping from Source.
A sad dismembered lonely vigil,
a lovers lost illusion,
a dream untrue.

The energy of sorrow is deep, still and dark.
It beckons like cold gusts on sunset waves
and melancholic purple petals stark.

When you sink into the sorrow card
see beyond the illusions.
Let blackness be your mirror
reflecting back your protecting love, joy and
reconnection live in this image.

Recognize eternity
as your balm and your pain;
your fleeting teacher.

Return into the only arms
ever to hold you;
the arms of universal love.

Fear

Seven of Cups

SEVEN OF CUPS

"FEAR"

Barnacle clinging mercilessly
to cups encrusted splendor
like octopus arms sucking blood.

Turn your heart towards the pressure;
turn and see disappearing illusions
as fear becomes an ally forcing
heart to open further,

When you face the Fear card,
advance towards your nemesis.

Gird yourself with *Strength* and
clear *Judgment.*
Allow Fear to clarify your path
—as Ally, NOT master—
of your *Chariot* emotions.

The energy of the Fear card
Is flowing and strong
deep yet illusory.

Ride your Fear
like a white stallion.
bravely into perceived
danger.

Stagnation

Eight of Cups

EIGHT OF CUPS

"STAGNATION"

Stagnation like old pot shards
in desert deep dark canyon caves
dusty useless, empty hard;
or like land held waters
in a spreading drought,
or thimble held tears
in emotional blight.

It is the dank musty scent
of the jaded, mossy forest floor;
of waters trapped and old
like emotions blocked at Future's door.

The energy of stagnation
is potent, bland
silty, shifting sand.
It is emotions resting
in deep cold waters
to awaken in sun drenched
bright-light, smiling land.

If you are stuck with the stagnation card
let your emotions sway and sit
in dark waters chilly lie,
waiting, but not too long
to bubble up
another day.

Fulfilment

Nine of Cups

NINE OF CUPS

"FULFILLMENT"

The emotion of the Hermit
explodes old caves and dusty paths;
winding up lofty slopes and wrapping
all in bounteous pearls
of abundance.

Deep red wines and crystal cups,
give homage to silent solitude,
rewarding inner richness,
with flowering
finery.

If you draw the Fulfillment card
prepare to accept manifested
gifts and rich wines bubbling up
from the depths of your wishes.

Fulfillment is your inner being hugging
your outer self,
with dreams fulfilled.

The energy of the Fulfillment card,
is resplendent and celebratory.

It is the endless shell of plenty,
pouring your finest dreams
into your life's cup.

Passion

Ten of Cups

TEN OF CUPS

"PASSION"

Passion bursts like bright red flowers
stampeding stamens in the wind,
pollen bursting in shimmering bliss
as frenzied need for future love.

Passion is emotional fortune;
like golden horned Leo goblet,
with rich honey dewy wine within,
bringing forth from tender
in quivering clasping match.

The energy of passion is vital, rich and syrupy.
Like honey flowing to an altar, to join anew,
or bees swarming flower pits in queen's
supplicant service.

Passion wells forth.

When you are struck by the passion card
prepare to meet the target of your hidden
love and blossom forth
in emotional enfolding.

Passion is your unbridled love
wresting you to your gardens
within.

WORLDS

Master

Sage of Worlds

SAGE OF WORLDS

"MASTER"

The Sage of Worlds is wise in his contentment.

He gracefully has spun his wheels
and now
in Masterful calm is finally released
from the spokes, rims, hubs
that his Karmic debts have settled.

Master is autumnal gold
and glowing bullion,

Master is the weaver of dreams
to share.

When you meet the "Master" card
you are summoned
to your highest craft
as an expression of your waiting
genius.

Reach high as attainment
awaits your reach.

The energy of the "Master" card
is calm and confident.
Master is wise and secure
in his great talent.
Master just does the work and assumes the stars
are coming to lift him again,
as always.

Player

Child of Worlds

CHILD OF WORLDS

"PLAYER"

Child of Worlds plays with life;
In fluid joy she skates its perils.
Fearless as a balloon
dancing the clouds;
Or swinging in a tube over treacherous waters
in blind attention to wind hissing over,
dangers adults wisely avoid.

Player is learning the transits of growth
as kittens plays with wool as prey,
or initiation rites of passage;
like Halo to return senses lost;
in video reality
grown into.

If the Player card picks you,
relax,
and return to unknown bravery.
Be the "chill dude" and "kewl" as fresh snow;
"Do it, just do it!"
as unplanned celebration
of living.

The energy of the Child of Worlds card
is jubilant and brave,
ignorantly wise and fresh,
unhindered by jaded knowing
of "Can't."

Preserver

Woman of Worlds

WOMAN OF WORLDS

"PRESERVER"

Woman of Worlds is full and nourishing.
Preserver is fecund in all ways.
She prepares by honoring what is;
creating a nest that the future can grow in.

Preserver honors the old
and births the new.
She takes the best and sweeps
the other.
Preserver dances life
into the unborn.

If you behold the Woman of Worlds card,
look at all that is valuable in your world,
then add to this with your mind, body and spirit.
Accentuate the positive
and the rest will fade.

The energy of the Preserver card is soft
and growing.
Woman of Worlds radiates
gentle strength,
by blending the best of the old with the new.

Preserver gives birth
to the Future.

Achiever

Man of Worlds

MAN OF WORLDS

"ACHIEVER"

Achiever flings aside the gates,
charging into his dreams unhindered
by doubt or restraint:
like a Ram he enters.

Man of Worlds makes his mark.

Success radiates out of him and flows into
his spirit, mind and emotions.
Achiever simply accepts his birthright,
knowing all the rewards his striving brings
as his fitting adornment.

When you earn the Achiever Card,
"Go for it!" is your trusting mantra.
With your dreams aligned and ordered,
the heavens will reward your toil
with unfettered Horns of Plenty.

The energy of the Achiever card
is glistening and bold;
gilded and pure.

Achiever quivers with anticipation,
and doubtless certainty.

Achiever Does and Gets!

Success

Ace of Worlds

ACE OF WORLDS

"SUCCESS"

After dragging emotions
through turbulent bitter trials
and Spirit beyond inner denials,
mind drives through
in endless motion
till here in body arrivals celebration;
the sought victory – success arrives!

The energy of success is exultant,
bubbling with compressed aims
released and plans long laid now
achieved.

Success is magnificent
manifestation in motion.
Focus rewarded.

When you win the success card,
redouble your efforts,
push your dreams.

Like waiting eggs
they will soon hatch
and joyful beaming
will engulf
your bursting smiles.

Success awaits
your determined action.

Reflection

Two of Worlds

TWO OF WORLDS

"REFLECTION"

Tranquil blue icing
like Priestess reflecting
cold and barren splendor,
like night Moon over ice
allows the past to return
embellished without
sentiment.

When you gaze at the Reflection card,
see your Past as a *Priestess* would;
be the hidden white fox and
blend easily into your memories,
let memories be your scenery,
both one.

Allow mind and world to join.

The energy of the Reflection card,
Is crisp and clear;
mirrored and cool.

The world of Reflection is as quiet
as a snowy step
and sharp as cracking ice.

Reflection takes you
back in.

Nurturing

Three of Worlds

THREE OF WORLDS

"NURTURING"

Holding loving tenderly
guarding growth fulfillment,
nurturing mother guards growth
like swallows on a nest warming
protected eggs in warm embrace.

The energy of nurturing is warm
and enveloping;
gentle as a trunk like young apples held
into the light,
growing from inner sap like rich milk
suckled from the brimming breast.

When you hold the nurturing card
prepare to hug and succor
in grooming licking love
allowing growth from
loving strength.

Nurturing allows the next
entry in the coddling nest
as Empress sharing kingdom
to the yet becoming.

Commencement

Four of Worlds

FOUR OF WORLDS

"COMMENCEMENT"

Commencement is the alpha of the rest
ramming through the stalling gates
like Emperor's will sternly saying "Go now!"
dismissing opposition or excuse
"Do it—just do it now—go!"

Martian willful warrior start
dismissing aeon's long wait.
In decisive beginning of a march
conquering indolent harsh stall
in drawing breath
and plunging on.

The energy of commencement
is decisive and clear.
It births in constant burst blowing
bewilderment away.

When you choose the commencement card,
waiting is done and plans unkempt
must burst through the fetid gates of indecision
and begin their rush to all paths and stones
towards their omega destination goal.

Go do it: start now.

Setback

Five of Worlds

FIVE OF WORLDS

"SETBACK"

Setback is as sudden as broken china.
Setback is hot winds blowing through dried husks
like dust grinding steel
into shards of rust.
Setback is a golden sunset
behind angry black clouds.

Setback is, however, but a
pause,
a brief halt
to forward motion.

Breathe in the pause and wrecks will be rebuilt
as a gleaming new style awaits you
beyond the temporary stop.

The energy of Setback is fleeting but bleak.
It sets plans adrift into whirling winds of doubt.
Setback forces rethinking into the bigger
and movement beyond the temporary.
Setback is a chance to realign into the now.

When the Setback card confronts you
see beyond the sudden dust and husks.
Rebuild your dreams anew.
Let drought take yesterday
into a gleaming new today.
The desert blooms brightest
after ravaging fires.
Allow your seeds to open
in the flames of setback.

Synergy

Six of Worlds

SIX OF WORLDS

"SYNERGY"

Synergy adds in multiples
making more from less
in loving symmetry blending
in twisting elegance
a perfect fit.

Lovers in the world allow
in compassionate understanding
and gently meld together
like bees to pollen flowering
or swans in loving frolicking.

The energy of Synergy
is soft and growing
gentle and strong
uniting to more
compounding with love.

When you receive the Synergy card
prepare to join talents
and become more than
any one can be alone.

Breakthrough

Seven of Worlds

SEVEN OF WORLDS

"BREAKTHROUGH"

Breakthrough is the switch,
the on from off,
the go from naught,
the cracking through,
the sudden yes
the "A ha" ness.

Lava bursts from pent
building pressured mount.
Like sprinters quivering
in holding for crack to release
like arrows from a bow
after long rest a quivered.

The Energy of breakthrough
is fiery and explosive;
stallions in a spring race
leaping finally through
the starting gate.

When you have the breakthrough card,
prepare for instant change and
chariot explosion
after silent wait.

Breakthrough is your cocoon bursting
and you
suddenly transformed and new.
Manifest your new in silence
burst forth as planned
anew.

Change

Eight of Worlds

EIGHT OF WORLDS

"CHANGE"

Change is as effortless as a chameleon,
as gentle as a golden leaf falling
or raindrops drawing buds
to sprout in autumnal sands.

The Energy of change is as sudden as a breeze,
as soft as silent snow,
as predictable as time.

When you encounter the change card
relax and drop all that was
and soften into new now.

Know that differences
will appear and colors will shift
but under shifting masks
all remains for always.

One is all and all is one
and closet clothes change
outer only.

Balance remains like dance
and universal chance
in whirling ever changing.

Harvest

Nine of Worlds

NINE OF WORLDS

"HARVEST"

Reap well earned providence;
gather
your corns of abundance.

Reflect and love
your joyous prescience.

Setting aside previous moderation
celebrate
the waiting bounty.

The energy of harvest
is bountifully rewarding.

It is a rich golden handshake
for Hermit's dedicated work.

It is feasting tables' delights.

When you reap the harvest card
cash in your chips
and enjoy your winnings.

Harvest is the luxurious picnic
after the climb.

A well deserved reward.

Reward

Ten of Worlds

TEN OF WORLDS

"REWARD"

Rejoice in autumnal gilded delights,
like golden creams and glistening bites;
crystal singing bubbles of golden cheer,
and beach walks with lovers highs
are Fortune's reward
for karmic tasks re-payed.

When rainbow lands on gilded stall
of market basket's overflowing
and bullion baubles dance in glistening cheer
or lush, green grass carpet under picnic clouds
and clean, fresh breeze wafts over portable feasts,
delight
with lovers deep eyed wonder,
at fate's deep wisdom sight.

The energy of the reward card is lush and expansive.
It glistens with pleasures and releases all constraint.

Reward card is the payback.
It says thank you from the all
and welcomes you as "I am"
into higher firmament.

When you earn the reward card
relax and breathe in delightful joy,
knowing it always was your birthright.

Celebrate your return
to remembrance.

WANDS

Seer

Sage of Wands

SAGE OF WANDS

"SEER"

Seer, like Owl, sees in darkness.
Parting the flaming veil
he is warmed by fire,
and sees through it
into beyond.

Seer chants and beats
in awakened trance,
using this life to plunge beyond.
Seer uses his wisdom to cut his earthy chains
and wander.

If you are guided by the Sage of Wands card,
prepare for an opening beyond
your normal senses.
Prepare for information to come
from your patient inner media;
winding its way
as inner knowing.

Trust it.
The energy of Sage of Wands is
fiery and pure,
old and deep,
gentle but strong.
The Seer is living revelation.
He is ancient,
collapsing paradigms.

He carries you in his talons
into flight.

Seeker

Child of Wands

CHILD OF WANDS

"SEEKER"

Seeker looks with trusting eyes.

He sees the wind rippling,
the tall, forest trees
shadowing
his tracks.

He hears the rabbit's ears twitching,
notices the doe's eyes
vigilant.

Child of Wands expects Spirit.
In constant communion,
she senses its deep mystery.

Seeker sits in silent mantras
chanting Spirit in sing song rhyme
simply trusting.

If you find the Seeker card,
drop into silence
and look for Spirit,
in your senses.

The energy of Child of Wands card
is young and fresh like sunrise;
as free as dandellion seeds
blowing in wind's warm embrace;
as enveloping as the mantra,

"Ohm Mani Padme Hum."

Sensor

Woman of Wands

WOMAN OF WANDS

"SENSOR"

Fingers rising from dancing trance,
Sensor feels beyond the sacred circle.
Sensor is as sensuous as a snake;
as filling as a deep breath on a cold morning;
as penetrating as an eclipse
on a sweet summer night.

Sensor closes her eyes to see.
Drum beats guide her beyond
into dimensions of touch.

Feeling creation molding
like clay to a potter,
she whirls beyond the wheel.

When you hold the Sensor card,
prepare for Woman of Wands
to take you beyond the here and
touch emotions of other beings.
Prepare to open
and see with inner sight.
Prepare to travel and grow.

The energy of Woman of Wands
is subtle and intense like incense.
It is a drumbeat, dwelving in and through.
It lifts silently like feathers;
peers beyond like black cats
with piercing, yellow eyes.

Actor

Man of Wands

MAN OF WANDS

"ACTOR"

The man of Wands dwells in Spirit,
peering through the Mask he holds.
Actor knows that mask shows his choice;
behind Eternal is the Man;
limitless as Soul.

Actor knows that the mask is his persona—
his current disguise which he role plays with.
Actor changes his costume effortlessly;
Actor flows with his being shifting
like chameleon.

When you play with the Actor card
look behind your shifting outer.
See who you always are and
imbue your personality
with magic.

The energy of the Actor is seriously fun.
Actor fills the stage with shamanic wisdom,
shape-shifting into your mind.

Actor gives you courage to change
identity.

Illumination

Ace of Wands

ACE OF WANDS

"ILLUMINATION"

Opal hand rests
on bands together meeting
iridescent wisdom blades of
firework splendor.

Instant karma born,
naked and waiting.

When you behold the Illumination card,
prepare for Magician to enter as
instant wisdom opens all doors and windows,
as you are ONE with all.

Allow the Universe to enter!

The energy of the Illumination card
is sparkling and fresh,
bright and new
flashing instantly within.

The Universe rests in bold knowing
like falling stars rising
into your heart.

Illumination opens you.

Purity

Two of Wands

TWO OF WANDS

"PURITY"

Purity is all that's left
when all that is not
has gone and rests
beyond the gleaming gates.

Purity is the cleansing quest,
the vibrating shaking entropy
reaching reaching reaching higher
to ever rarer limbs where angel wings
give flight towards angelic sights
and all that angel eyes can bring.

The energy of purity is gently stern
relentlessly purging toxic clean
like footsteps in the virgin snow
or elephant ears hearing all below
beyond the monster footstep blows.

If you are cleansed by the purity card
allow priestess wings to take you high
beyond candlelight sight
or snake track sandy worming trek.
Climb your corporeal mountain peak
and see above frosty gleaming heights
as clear vibrating bright.
Purity is your lotus flower,
your concrete cracking power.
Determination driving always up
beyond the muddy, slimy soup
to bring the heaven in your mind,
before you polished, pure and kind.

Compassion

Three of Wands

THREE OF WANDS

"COMPASSION"

Breathing in and breathing out
bellows balancing fiery winds
as all being in each
and each in the other.

Compassion as fire
brings one to all.

Seeing others as different
sets us within
and binds to same.

The Energy of three
is gentle as an Empress's wand;
as sweet as an infant swan;
as vital as a fire cracking seeds
to future forest sapling's spread.

When you are gifted with the compassion card
prepare for winds of soft spirit
to crack your selfish husk
and merge you into the one
forest of humanity and more.

Compassion is the soft breath
of spirit breathing in your ear,
"love the other
he is you."

Aspiration

Four of Wands

FOUR OF WANDS

"ASPIRATION"

Reaching for the heavens,
the Emperor sends his spirit
with deep conviction to above
to draw down in reverent love
his future path unleavened
as pure intended spirit-ation.

Creating from the wanting
material from ethereal being
like llamas circling a rising fist
or wishes walking out of mist
below as above becomes
aspiration created.

The energy of aspiration
is insistent as a gust of wind
inevitable as a changing season
asking as receiving
just becomes
just because
you asked.

When you have the aspiration card
with no doubt ask and reach above
then by waiting with imperial patience
watch it come adorned
in the glittering gowns
of heaven.

Oppression

Five of Wands

FIVE OF WANDS

The ghost of oppression
is like a dark cloud
enshrouding all
in its barred barb delusion.

It is a free flying falcon caught in nets
and put in metal shackles.

Oppression traps the open
in gullible delusions of rope.

Oppression is a crystal without light.

The energy of oppression
is delusional but thick,
trapping all who doubt
in its cast iron prison
and dungeons of brick.

When Oppression corners you,
turn your mind to light.
See the shackles melting
in thoughts turned open.

When you release the falcon of your mind
you will fly as one,
beyond.

Follow your heart above
and you will be free.

Trust

Six of Wands

SIX OF WANDS

"TRUST"

Beyond gravity hangs
whirling dancers high
knowing trust making
easy flight beyond the sky.

Trust beyond belief
puts lives on line
and leaping grasps
holding hands share
like candles lit in rain.

The energy of trust is gentle and strong.
Trust is our bedrock knowing
like eagle chick leaping from the heights
or braving nine months of darkness
waiting for breath.

When you accept the trust card
go forth together and know
you are held as puzzle part
indispensable to all.

Trust is one with meaning;
the loving Spirit holding all
together onwards ever
forever up.

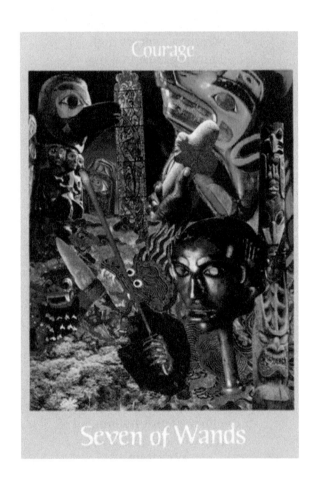

Courage

Seven of Wands

SEVEN OF WANDS

"COURAGE"

When the mask of fear is ripped away
only courage remains guarding all we are.

Go forth and seek out your fears.
Find their dark dragon faces,
and without mortal concerns,
attack them all
with Damascus's steely might.

When we slay fear,
we become the guardian knights
of main street,
guiding others beyond
their own dark nights,
into their becoming.

The energy of courage is primal.
We are being by becoming.

Face limitations with unflinching clarity
and sharp determination
and ever growing love of all.

Let Courage be your steady gaze
in your mirror of truth.
Push beyond your staid, complacent paradigm
ever into more.

Courage finds endless energy
in its eternal quest:
join it!

Harmony

Eight of Wands

EIGHT OF WANDS

"HARMONY"

Harmony is spiritual balance,
like the sound of violin chords
weaving through a bamboo forest
or flute note echoing through canyon walls.

Harmony keeps Soul in balance.

Harmony's Mother is *Balance 8*.
His siblings are *Synthesis*, *Stagnation* and *Change*.
Together they walk the tight rope;
together they dance towards Infinity.

When you listen to the Harmony card,
expect pure musical notes
and rainbows on your path.
Harmony will balance your pangs
like trumpets calling from above.

The energy of the Harmony card
is soft and sweet, like honey,
enveloping like a spring breeze,
exhilarating as a surfer's wave.

Harmony is as penetrating
as a drumbeat
on a desert morning.

Integrity

Nine of Wands

NINE OF WANDS

"INTEGRITY"

Integrity is the deepest soul of the Hermit
on lonely vigil searching
for Spirit on the lofty mountains,
or the cathedral rose glass spires,
or ancient stone obelisks,
and finding resonance,
silent and alone.

Integrity beckons from within.

The energy of integrity is stark and rich
like deep blue silk carpeting rocky paths
or backbone curves holding
us upright
in silent trust.

When the the integrity card challenges you,
prepare for silent clouds
of laden moral being.
You inner flocks of birds
will fly as one,
but alone in a bustling crowd.

Integrity beckons from within,
like minaret cries in desert skies,
drawing us forth.

Growth

Ten of Wands

TEN OF WANDS

"GROWTH"

Growth is subtle and strong.
It is vine that winds up your spine.
Brave, like light, growth
looks in the cracks,
forces out the mildew of doubt,
brightens the gaps within
bridges strength.

If you rise to meet the Growth card,
expect to shift higher
and weakness to transform,
into strengths beyond doubt
as Fortune's spirit awakens you.

The energy of Growth is pervasive.
Like light, it is eternal and deep.

Growth is as young as a flower,
as old as a stone tree ring.

Growth is strong like morning dew,
cracking a granite tor
with loving expansion.

Growth is life
celebrating itself.

ACKNOWLEDGEMENTS

Life in a way is like a spring shower. Drops, puddles and cascading water drench our experience and add fragrance and purpose to our life's journey. In the warm afterglow of the spring sun we grow. So too my life, and whatever I can share from it would be incomplete without all those who have nurtured me. I honor all who have crossed my path and showered me with their passing essence, love and wisdom. I thank you all and I pray that I have added in some way to yours.

Thanks to Patricia Diorio who showed me the magic of Voyager Tarot almost twenty years ago. She was the first to teach me how to access Spirit's profound wisdom and beauty through Tarot. She showed me that a life spent in service to Spirit was not only possible but rich, beautiful and real.

I'd like to thank Susan Shapiro who lovingly and wisely coached and guided me to believe that I could live a creatively abundant life with and by Tarot. By creating my beautiful web site, she gave me a foundation on which to build it.

Thank you Treysii Zamorano who strongly and lovingly guided my growth through using Facebook and other 21st century media to set up a strong web presence and also encouraged my tarot poems to help achieve that. She was the one who first suggested that I explore each card via poetry which led eventually to this book.

Special thanks to my dear friend Emalani Malea who repeatedly told me that the poems should be published. Her dynamic connection to Spirit showed me how important language is in all its forms: it connects humanity to their spiritual core.

Thank you Amy Beth Katz, my editor and the publisher of *Living Dreams Press* for believing in me and the value of these poems. She gently and lovingly pushed and prodded me, confidently and constantly trusting in our partnership and in this book.

Most important for me was the deep influence and witty wisdom of my magnificent teacher and friend James Wanless. I would not be the professional Tarot guide and poet if not for him and his wonderful deck. Thank you, dear James, for this precious gift. You have enriched all who use it.

When I look back and see the crevasses, cliffs and meadows of my climb up towards the mountain peak of this project, I remember, honor and thank all those whom guided me onwards—often unknowingly. The people in the following list and those already mentioned have been among the most influential to me. I started this list with the intention of honoring 78 dear ones, one for each card/poem. That number turned out to be insufficient. I began the process of dedications by focusing on each person: their energy and my gratitude for all they have blessed me with. I then blindly drew a card, in the tradition of Tarot, asking Spirit for guidance as to which card/poem best encapsulates our relationship and the gifts within them.

The accompanying poem is an important part of the message. Apart from my family, they are not in any order. I suggest you take the card and poem as one together; as my humble offering.

Many Thanks and Love to You All,

~ Lloyd

Fortune: **Dave H.**
Compassion: **Dagmar H.**
Change: **Del H.**
Growth: **Lani Z.**
Stagnation: **Jennie D.;
Mike G.; Linda S.**
Negativity: **Shelley Z**
Priestess: **David Z.**
Rejoicer: **Tom Z.**
Feeler: **Joanie S.**
Regenerator: **Marcia D.**
Integrity: **Starr C.**
Commencement: **Karen J.**
Inventor: **Anna Marie S.**
Sensor: **Pat P.**
Sorrow: **Dick C.**
Seeker: **Preben F.**
Reward: **Fred X.**
Time Space: **Virginia W.;
Dennie L.**
Equilibrium: **John L.;
Haze W.**
Universe: **James F.**
Success: **Peter W.; Billy T.**
Fear: **Ruhr P.; Helene W.**
Courage: **Don M.; Martha
G; Randal R.; Joanna L**
Oppression: **Helen M.**
Breakthrough: **Susie
F.;Tom AA.**
Confusion: **Vickie B.**
Devil's Play: **Isabel R.**
Hermit: **Fiona B.**
Logic: **Jane S.**
Synthesis: **Steve S.**
Creativity: **Uta K.**
Achiever: **Raymond P.**
Setback: **Peter R.**
Moon: **Gordon L.**
Delusion: **Reggie D.;
Vivienne Y.**
Disappointment: **Dave D.**
Purity: **Barbara S.**
Harmony: **John S.**

Nurturing: **Will H.**
Harvest: **Pamela J.**
Lovers: **Rich M.**
Passion: **Richard S.**
Aspiration: **Unity TM.**
Anger: **Jake B.**
Strength: **Valerie V.**
Illumination: **Jennifer J.**
Magician: **Christine C.**
Narrowness: **Naomi S.;
Izzie X.**
Brilliance: **Jeremy B.**
Preserver: **Heidi P.**
Player: **Ron S.**
Ecstasy: **Alison S.**
Equanimity: **Joei S.**
Fulfillment: **James H.**
Fool Child: **Mary G.**
Chariot: **Tommy T.**
Emperor: **Jay L.**
Synergy: **Eileen N.**
Seer: **Sally H.**
Death: **Eldon E.**
Guardian: **Andoni L.**
Love: **Jack A.**
Hanged Man: **Mike O.**
Dullness: **Alec J.**
Star: **Dusty R.; Jim C.**
Master: **Don V.**
Tower: **Nikki B.**
Hierophant: **Trampas G.**
Surfer: **Andrew S.**
Empress: **Joyous H.**
Knower: **Kiyoko S.**
Balance: **Katherine S.**
Trust: **Eirwen M.**
Reflection: **Rob C.**
Learner: **Karen T.**
Art: **Zareena Z.**
Sun: **Melani K.; Fatah E.;
Nancy K.**
Actor: **Garrett M.;
Bernard K.**

ABOUT THE AUTHOR

R. Lloyd Hegland is a poet, Tarot reader, tour guide and public speaker in sunny Santa Barbara. He loves "Life, people, Gaia and the wonderful Spirit which flows through and blends them all so beautifully."

In addition to Tarot readings, which he offers in person and via phone, Lloyd writes personalized tarot poems, and is available for talks, readings, weddings and other group events. He will soon be merging his two most recent vocations in the exciting new "Tarot-Tours" which blends travel with Tarot.

Along with living out his soul's calling, Lloyd recently drew the "Lovers" card and is ready to meet his Soul Mate.

For further information email Lloyd at:
lloyd@onthepathtarot.com

and visit his website:
www.onthepathtarot.com

**THESE BOOKS AND MORE ARE AVAILABLE
AS INSTANT PDF DOWNLOADS
AT LIVING DREAMS PRESS**

Voyager Tarot Companion
by R Lloyd Hegland

How to Become An Extraordinary Psychic
by Debra Lynne Katz

Freeing the Genie Within
by Debra Lynne Katz

Writing With the Infinite Spirit
by Carol Batey

What's Cooking In Your Soul
by Carol Batey

The Lizard Thieves: Love Poems
by Amy Beth Katz

Living Dreams Press
www.livingdreamspress.com

CPSIA information can be obtained at www.ICGtesting.com
Printed in the USA
LVOW02s0346260515

439872LV00012B/187/P